The
Hare-Shaped Hole

Brimming with creative inspiration, how-to projects, and useful information to enrich your everyday life, Quarto is a favourite destination for those pursuing their interests and passions.

The Hare-Shaped Hole © 2023 Quarto Publishing plc
Text © 2023 John Dougherty. Illustrations © 2023 Thomas Docherty

First published in 2023 by Frances Lincoln Children's Books, an imprint of The Quarto Group. The Old Brewery, 6 Blundell Street, London N7 9BH, United Kingdom.
T (0)20 7700 6700 F (0)20 7700 8066
www.Quarto.com

A catalogue record for this book is available from the British Library.

ISBN 978-0-7112-7605-5

The illustrations were created digitally.
Set in Filosofia

Published by Peter Marley
Edited by Hattie Grylls
Designed by Ness Wood
Production by Dawn Cameron

Manufactured in Guangdong, China TT102022

10 9 8 7 6 5 4 3 2 1

FSC
www.fsc.org
MIX
Paper from responsible sources
FSC® C016973

For Noah and Cara, as always and ever.
For Lauren and Georgie, just because.
And most of all for Jen, who loved Bertle and Hertle first. - J.D.

In memory of Cadi - T.D.

John Dougherty   ✳   Thomas Docherty

The Hare-Shaped Hole

Frances Lincoln
Children's Books

Bertle and Hertle were always a pair

though one was a turtle and one was a hare.

They were utterly buddies, and best friends forever,

and whenever you looked, you would find them together.

You might think their
friendship was doomed
to disaster,
for Bertle was slower
and Hertle was faster

while Hertle was never
at home in the water,
no matter the number
of tips Bertle taught her.

But Hertle was patient, and Hertle was kind,
so Hertle would never leave Bertle behind;
and if Hertle Hare never learned how to swim,
well, Bertle was there and she counted on him.

"I'm so glad you're my buddy! So glad you're my friend!
It's you and me, always! We're friends to the end!"

They both used to say this.
They both felt the same.
　　　Until, quite unexpectedly …

　　　… the end came.

One day, there were two of them,
turtle and hare.
The next day: poor Bertle!
His friend wasn't there.

She just wasn't there.
There was nothing to see

but a hole in the air
where a hare ought to be.

Bertle at first thought
it couldn't be true.
When his friend disappears,
what's a turtle to do?

So he searched high and low,
and he searched far and wide.

He looked all round the hole,
and he looked deep inside.

He looked in the stream,
and he looked underground.
She was nowhere he looked.
She was not to be found.

And the only reminder
she'd ever been there
was a cold, empty,
Hertle-shaped hole in the air.

Then Bertle got angry.
He quite lost control
and he shouted,

"I hate you, you

So leave me
alone!

Go get lost!

Go away!"

horrible hole!

But a hole's just a hole.
It had nothing to say.

And it hung there beside him, a constant reminder
that Hertle had gone, and that no one could find her.

His voice hoarse and raw, Bertle started to plead,
"Tell me, hole in the air – is there something you need?
If I give you my toys, if I'm good every day,
will you bring Hertle back? And will *you* go away?"

But the hole simply hung there, all empty and black.
It did not go away.

Nor did Hertle come back.

Then Bertle the turtle felt weak with despair,
alone with this cold, empty hole in the air.
He let out a sob, and then, with a shiver,
sat miserably down on the bank of the river.

And there, without Hertle the hare by his side,
he cried, and he cried, and he cried,
and he cried. He felt sorrow seize him,
and sadness surround him …

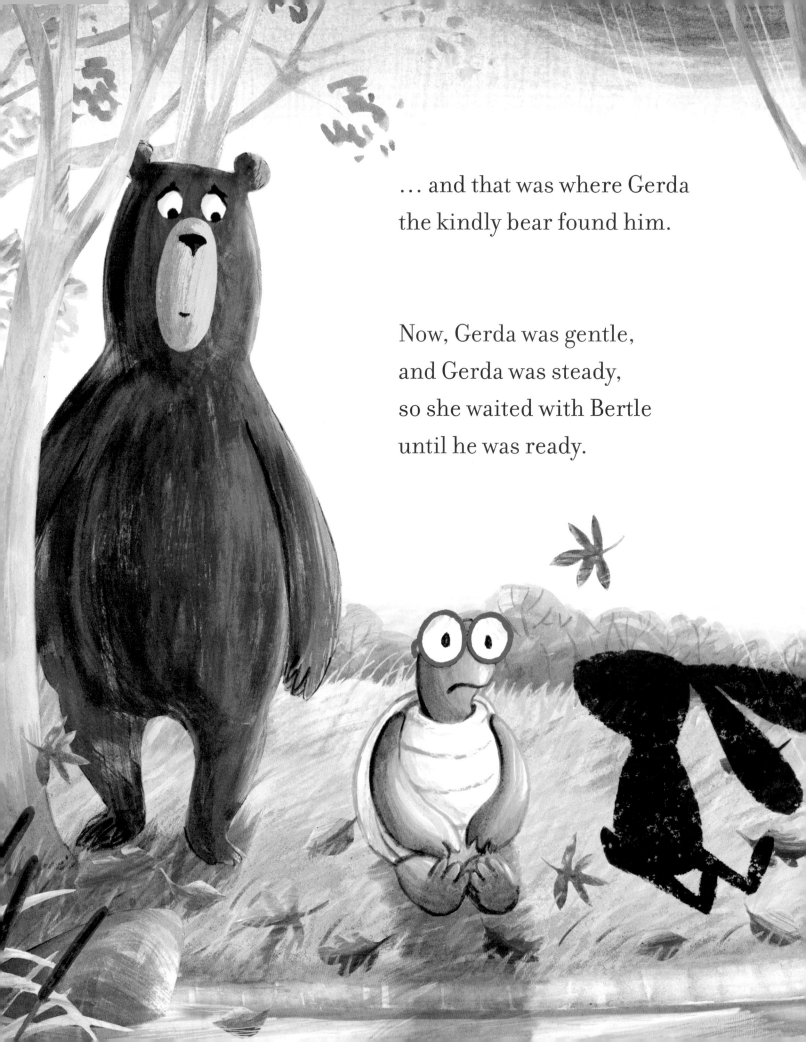

… and that was where Gerda
the kindly bear found him.

Now, Gerda was gentle,
and Gerda was steady,
so she waited with Bertle
until he was ready.

She cuddled that small turtle-child as he cried
and let him feel all he was feeling inside.

Till at last Bertle said, with a sad little cry,
"Why did she have to go, Gerda Bear? Why?
And why is this horrible hole in the air
here to remind me that Hertle's not there?"

Then he felt Gerda sigh, and he felt Gerda stir,
and she said, as he buried his face in her fur,
"Little Bertle, I'm old – so much older than you.
Let me tell you some things that I know to be true."

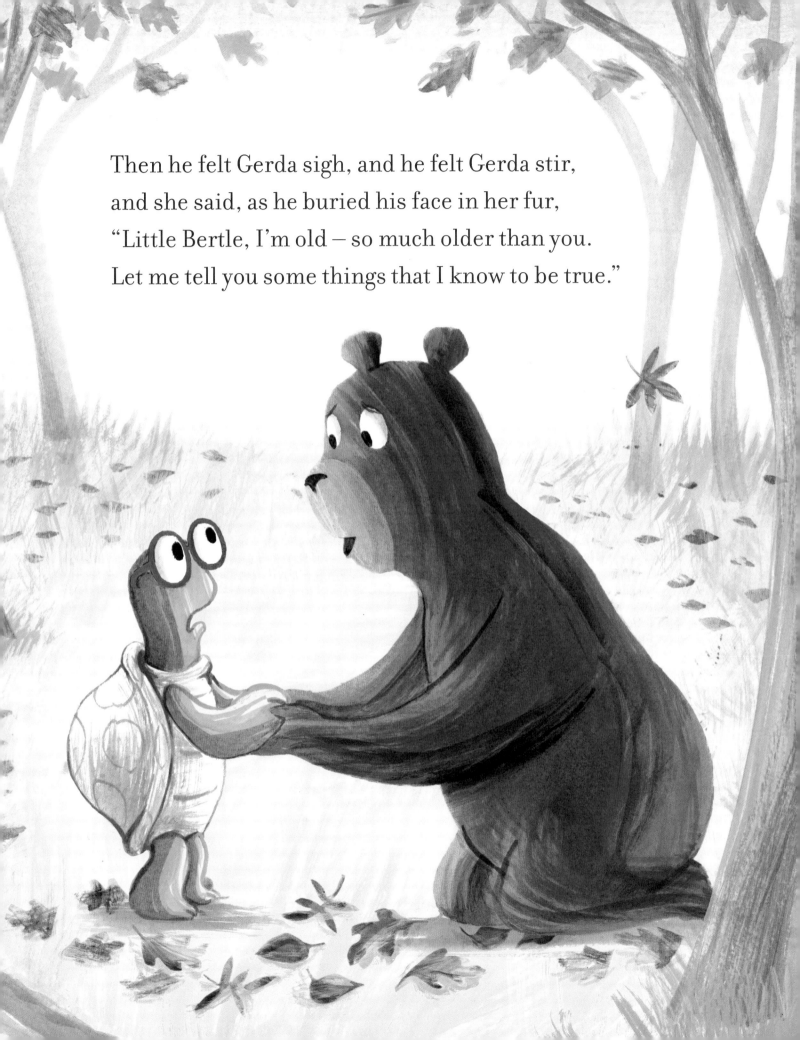

"Life is not always happy. You'll find, as you grow,
that sometimes a person you love has to go.
Sometimes they move away. Sometimes, they die.
And sometimes, they leave without saying goodbye.

There's no getting rid of this hole in the air.

If you take away nothing, well, nothing's still there.

You can't just ignore it, or lose it, or hide it.

Instead, you can fill it. Put something inside it."

"Think of all of the things
you and Hertle have done.
All the games you have played.
All the ways you've had fun.

All the times you each helped
and supported and shared.
All the dozens of ways that
she showed you she cared.

Then speak out those memories!
Speak them out loud!
Let the emptiness know that
you're grateful and proud …

… to have known her. It's hard,
but I'll help you begin it.
Speak those memories into
the hole. Put them in it."

It was hard, to begin with,
but as Bertle spoke,
his memories of Hertle's
bright friendship awoke.

And, telling the hole why
he'd never forget her,
he slowly began
to feel …

… just a bit better.

Then Gerda said, "Now — take your memories home.
They'll help you whenever you're sad and alone.

From the first of the year
till the last of December,
keep them close by your side.
And always:

  remember."

Bertle stood still, and he thought for a while.
And then, with a nod, and a sad little smile,
he hugged his friend Gerda.
He turned around

and ...

... he went home with his memories,

hand in hand.